Reverse Appliqué
WITH NO BRAKEZ

Jan Mullen

C&T PUBLISHING

© 2003 Jan Mullen

Editor-in-Chief: Darra Williamson

Editor: Cyndy Lyle Rymer

Technical Editor: Karyn Hoyt-Culp

Copyeditor/Proofreader: Laura M. Reinstatler/Carol Barrett/
Stacy Chamness

Design Director/Book Designer: Christina D. Jarumay

Cover Designer: Christina D. Jarumay

Illustrator: Kate Reed

Production Assistants: Kristy Konitzer and Luke Mulks

Photography: Bewley Shaylor unless otherwise noted

Published by C&T Publishing, Inc., P.O. Box 1456, Lafayette,
California 94549

Front cover: *Specimen Daisy* by Jan Mullen (see page 53)

Back cover: *Warm Spotz* by Jan Mullen (see page 61)

K Is for Kitty by Jan Mullen (see page 61)

Attention Teachers: C&T Publishing, Inc. encourages you to use this
book as a text for teaching. Contact us at 800-284-1114 or
www.ctpub.com for more information about the C&T Teachers
Program.

Library of Congress Cataloging-in-Publication Data

Mullen, Jan.
    Reverse appliqué with no brakez / Jan Mullen.
        p. cm.
Includes index.
  ISBN 1-57120-200-5 (paper trade)
  1. Appliqué–Patterns. 2. Machine quilting. 3. Quilts. I. Title.
  TT779 .M855 2003
  746.44'5–dc21
                                            2002014927

Printed in China
  0 9 8 7 6 5 4 3 2 1

DEDICATION

to my mum and dad
Betty and Bob Wood—
always encouraging and proud of us

ACKNOWLEDGMENTS

To Ben, who copes increasingly well with my absences and workload. I owe you a few Monday nights.

To Brodie, Keelan, and Miffy, who seem to manage very well when I'm not around to mother them, but who still look forward in anticipation to the (increasingly rare) home-cooked delights.

To Bewley, who—as usual—kept me working happily in the dark.

To my favorite editor, Cyndy Rymer, and the team at C&T, for their expert skills and continued confidence in me. I only work with nice people.

To Melodie, for feeding me the fabric while I stitched, and to Sally, who kept the paperwork under control while the machine was devouring fabric upstairs.

To Faye, Stephanie, Beth, and all at Marcus Brothers who have helped me produce much of the fabric used throughout this book.

To my students, who educate me as much as I do them. I am ever grateful for your contributions.

I raise my glass to you all.

Co n x e

PREFACE

We all have simple thoughts; some disappear and some stay just that—simple. Then there are those simple thoughts that turn out to be special: those that can be nurtured to grow quietly under control, and those we feed well that then take on a life of their own.

My interest in reverse appliqué came from one such simple, **special** thought...

Scratching Back to Our Beginnings by Jan Mullen, 51" x 37½", 1997

I've always been involved in art and tend to put my creative twist on everything I do. So it is no surprise that one day, quite a few years ago, as I tried to remember my first "art" experience, my mind wandered back to my childhood. Memories of color flooded back. Remember crayon resist? You must have done it: Heavy strokes of bright crayons completely covering the thick paper, then obliterated with heavy black paint. We were able to experience the carefree fun of color before joyfully slapping on paint to cover up the crayon and make our "secret." Finally, what pure delight to scratch through the paint to reveal a glorious surprise of color and pattern underneath!

Excited, my thoughts drifted quickly to the themes and images in childhood artwork: hearts, houses, family, friends, pets, play, and the key elements of life outdoors. These are also the symbols many of us work with as artists and quiltmakers. Our lives still revolve around those things so close to home and so close to us. I realized I had a simple, wandering thought to be quietly nurtured, and not surprisingly, as with some of my best thoughts, there was a quilt in it!

Even before I took up pencil and paper to sketch the design, I had in mind the look I wanted (primitive and happy), and the type of fabrics that would help me produce this look (brightly colored leftover silks and taffetas contrasted with a flat black). I also had a wealth of childhood/quilters' images to pick from floating free in

my brain. How then to put it all together to best achieve the result I wanted? Reverse appliqué was the obvious choice, with rough-cut, strip-pieced scraps for the under layer to represent the crayon layer, and with a single piece of black fabric for the top layer to represent the paint.

This technique seemed to suit me perfectly. As with everything I do, there had to be a twist. With this quilt, it was both the unusual scrap-pieced "secret" layer and the primitive look of the reverse appliqué.

As sometimes happens, one good thought leads to another. One good quilt also leads to another, and soon there was a second quilt. By taking those early thoughts further, and feeding them well, I have come up with so many options for variation that I would be happy to stop thinking for a while so I could explore this territory in greater detail!

Before long, popular demand had me teaching a class. All of these developments are an unintentional aside, a nice diversion from my usual occupation of designing "crooked" machine-pieced blocks with Stargazey Quilts. I feel sure that for you, another quiltmaker or fabric-and-thread devotee, the potential of reverse appliqué can only add a similar pleasant aside to your creative life. Maybe you'll be encouraged to nurture some simple thoughts too?

INTRODUCTION
The Secret Life of Reverse Appliqué

In its simplest form, reverse appliqué consists of layering two fabrics, and then cutting through the top layer to reveal the hidden layer underneath. The cut edges are then held down with stitches.

You may be familiar with the molas made by South American craftspeople. I am most familiar with the method that uses solid-colored fabrics and includes a multitude of hidden layers underneath. These hidden layers are usually exposed in what I like to think of as an "echo" or "ripple" effect, similar to the effect created by a stone dropped in the middle of a pond.

In the case of the fabric mola, new ripples of color are gradually exposed in layers moving outward to the edges of the design. The designs are usually intricate, and the method of appliqué is a traditional, invisible appliqué stitch.

The sample shown here was given to me by a student who explored the Darien Gap region of Panama in 1986. This piece was the bodice of a dress that she exchanged for some of her western gear. It seems to employ both reverse appliqué and appliqué: The yellow base and the red fabrics are whole, while most of the others appear to be inserted under or added on in smaller pieces. The result is an intricate design, but without the multitude of heavy layers.

Reverse appliqué from the Darien Gap region of Panama

While I have enormous appreciation for this type of work, I have no interest in replicating them, either in their design or their technique. Beautiful and fascinating as they are, it's just not the way I like to work.

Then how do I like to work and what makes my reverse appliqué so different?

I tend to put my imprint on whatever I create, and I love to encourage others to do the same. My style of piecing and quilting generally is a bit offbeat: not precise, but skewed and rather free. This book continues that tendency, but the designs are no longer restricted by the straight edges of machine piecing. Reverse appliqué offers me a way to execute designs that aren't easily adaptable to block-based patchwork and straight stitches.

Here, as in my normal patchwork style, strips—if I use them—are cut tapered, not straight. I use my cut-loose methods (from *Cut-Loose Quilts*, C&T, 2001) if I am making traditional-looking blocks for my secret or top layers, and, as usual, I prefer to relax traditional "rules" and work hard on the color and design.

So, with my style as a basis, we'll take apart the layers of a reverse-appliqué "quilt" and explore the options of each layer or process. I'll give you plenty of ideas and prompts, but ultimately it will be up to you to combine the various elements in your own work.

Chapter One takes you through the tools and equipment you may need. In reversing terms, we're packing the tool kit.

Chapter Two offers you the technical information you'll need to construct the different layers, from how to appliqué, to how to set up a floating border. Consider this the instruction manual. All the how-to is here so the later chapters can flow in a more inspirational vein.

We'll move to working out your design in Chapter Three, mapping the terrain, and plotting our journey. Sometimes this is the most daunting exercise for quilters, but I will offer you plenty of inspiration for subject matter, and show you how to vary the simplest of designs for added interest.

Sample-filled Chapters Four through Seven take you through the layers: the secret layer, the top layer, exposing the secret layer, and finishing. Here we pack our bags with the "underwear" and "overcoat"...and then reverse until we reach the end of our journey. Most of the samples in these chapters are made with a variation of my basic reversing style, which features a pieced scrappy layer that is hand appliquéd with embroidery floss (in the same color as the top layer), and machine quilted (also in the same color as the top layer). I've kept this as a constant throughout the chapters to showcase the differences in each highlighted technique. You may notice also that in these four chapters the samples are themed; I've chosen simple images that are easy to vary, which—not surprisingly—were seen in my first reversing quilt!

The projects in Chapter Eight illustrate a variety of techniques, styles, and methods of working that combine different options from the various chapters. Think of these as road trips; they certainly take you to interesting places! You may follow them exactly, or—in the spirit of "Stargazey style"—tweak them, alter them drastically, or simply read through them to reinforce the processes of working in different ways.

The final chapter features the gallery, which showcases a selection of student work in a variety of styles, subject matter, fabrics, and techniques. Consider it an overview of what you can achieve with even a minimum of instruction. In reversing terminology, this has to be a great record of journeys taken, an inspiring collection of postcards.

My samples appear throughout the book, and are worked in my personal style and color palette. Viewing them may open your eyes further still; perhaps one of these quilts will set your brain whizzing!

You may start your journey into reverse appliqué by following the basic process instructions, and taking ownership by picking a technique from each chapter. Perhaps you will launch yourself into reverse gear by making one of the projects, following my instructions closely but varying the palette and drawing up your own variation on the design. You may even get going with small back steps by incorporating just one simple idea into another of your own in-progress quilts.

Wherever you start, I am confident I will leave you inspired. So hold on tight, as you're about to take a joyride with me.

We're heading off down the road and we're reversing with no brakez.

Yippeeee!

CHAPTER 1

Tools

or packing the tool kit

We don't necessarily need a lot of fancy equipment to get started in this technique. Probably the best advice I can offer is to keep everything simple at the start, though if we're going to "burn rubber" in this neighborhood, it's great to know what's needed for every contingency.

I'll run you through what I find useful, but feel free to swap tools. We'll look at fabrics and threads in each of the following chapters.

A Peek into the Tool Kit

Depending on your project, you will need a varying array of tools and equipment. This is a list of what I used in making the examples in this book.

Rotary cutter, mat, and ruler. Use these to cut fabric for all layers. They are essential for cutting tapered strips for the secret layer and for trimming any secret-layer blocks ready for piecing.

Sewing machine. I use mine for piecing the secret layer, for machine quilting, and also for machine appliqué. You'll need different presser feet for these processes. I use a patchwork foot for general piecing, a quilting/darning foot for machine quilting and free-motion reverse appliqué, a walking foot for straight in-the-ditch stitching on big quilts, and an embroidery/ general foot for reverse appliquéing with programmed stitches.

Iron and ironing board. Essential for pressing all those seams, and for keeping the layers fresh and flat.

Scissors. You'll need two pairs: one for fabric and one for paper.

Thread clippers. I prefer these to scissors for cutting away the top layer to expose the secret layer underneath. There is less chance of cutting more than desired. They are also good for clipping seams and cutting threads!

Craft blade and mat. I use the craft blade for cutting stencils and also for cutting the top layer that has been prepared with fusible web. It takes a bit of practice to become proficient with a craft blade, but the results are well worth it.

Paper. You'll want smaller sheets for thumbnail sketches and larger sheets for full-size cartoons or stencils.

Permanent markers. You'll find one that marks a heavy line helpful for determining the areas to cut and for working out "bridges" when you are making stencils. A finer felt-tipped pen is helpful for transferring designs.

Template plastic. This is handy for making templates when you are working in a small repeat design.

Silver pencil, chalk wheel, or other fabric marker. Use these for marking the cutting/reversing lines on the top layer.

Safety pins. Size 00 brass pins are my preference for holding the sandwich together before preparing the appliqué, and later before quilting. Larger pins don't hold the sandwich as firmly and may leave unsightly holes in the top layer.

Appliqué and other pins. I prefer pins as small and slender as possible for holding down turned edges of the appliqué. Larger pins can catch the thread and also, when used profusely, shrink and distort the sandwich. I strongly suggest you place the pins perpendicular to the edge of the appliqué when pinning. The action of inserting the pin also pushes the top layer fabric allowance under, which is a bonus with reverse appliqué. I also use a variety of larger dressmaker's and quilter's pins, when needed, to hold fabrics together.

Needles. Hand-appliqué needles need to be sized to fit your thread. I choose the thinnest, sharpest one I can to enable a smooth glide through the fabrics. (I also look for the smallest eye possible, although it may be harder to thread!) The trick to pleasant stitching is to find the correct proportion. The thread, which is doubled through the eye, should slip easily through the hole made by the needle.

Here's a little trick for threading bulky embroidery floss: Thread half the number of strands needed, but double their length, then tie both sets of ends together. Six strands are much easier to pull through the fabric than twelve strands!

Thimbles and needle-grabbers. I need them to keep my poor fingers soft. Needle-grabbers are a help when pulling stubborn threads through the fabric too. Working the appliqué the way I do is not a delicate process!

Double-sided fusible web. This can be useful if your design is elaborate or if you are working with raw edges; use it on the reverse side of the top layer. I've also used this product when I am working with raw-edged scraps in the secret layer; it helps to stick them to the batting. Be aware that this does make the fabric stiffer, a quality that can be either an advantage or disadvantage.

Lightbox. This is helpful if you need to transfer accurate images, although I've managed with a window for years!

Cotton batting. I prefer a needle-punched variety. I always appliqué with an incomplete quilt sandwich as it keeps the layers flat and stable. Wash or steam-iron it first if you are worried about shrinkage; cotton batting does that! Also, if you have problems with bearding (the batting may come up with the stitches to the top layer), try using a sharper needle or skimming over the batting rather than stabbing up and down through it.

Masking tape. Useful for preparing a quilt sandwich and holding blocks together when using my quilt-as-you-go method on page 19.

That's one full bag we've packed!

CHAPTER 2

Technicalities

or the instruction manual

In this chapter I have gathered diverse technical information that will help you to appliqué, fuse, frame, sash, machine quilt, and bind your work. Not the most exciting area of the book, but don't skip it. This is as formal as I ever get and it's essential info!

Before we begin, let me illustrate what our sandwich is made of.

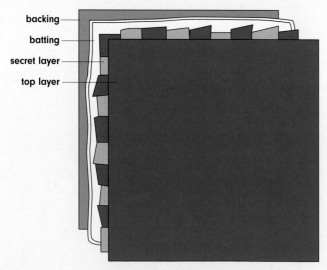

The reversing sandwich

backing
batting
secret layer
top layer

Variations of the top and secret layers appear in forthcoming chapters, but it is important to note from the start that I always work directly on a base of cotton batting. This gives a lovely, firm foundation for stitching and alleviates the need for a hoop.

If I am hand stitching I don't aim to appliqué right through the batting, but merely to catch it occasionally; the batting is there to prevent the grain of the fabric from being stretched. If I am machine appliquéing, the stitches go through the batting, of course!

I also usually omit the final backing until I am ready to quilt as I don't want it held at this stage—by hand or machine stitches. I use a temporary backing to keep my clothes from getting covered with batting fluff if I am hand stitching, or omit a backing completely while working the machine appliqué. When the appliqué is complete, I add the final backing to complete the sandwich, and I can proceed with quilting.

The Basic Process of Reversing with No Brakez

What follows is the basic process for reversing with no brakez. Refer back to the illustration of the reversing sandwich on page 14 as needed. Note that you can modify the basic process at any or all stages. We'll spend more time on this in Chapters Three through Seven.

1. Draw your design, to scale if necessary.

2. Gather the necessary fabrics and threads.

3. Cut a piece of batting somewhat larger than the design area. How large depends on how flexible you want to be with your design, and whether you have plans for borders and binding. Allow at least an inch all around to compensate for any shrinkage due to quilting, and to make finishing easier.

4. Cut a secret layer the same size as the batting. This may be pieced or composed using any of the methods described in the chapters that follow.

5. Lay the freshly pressed secret layer right side up on the batting.

6. Cut and/or piece the top layer.

7. Lay the freshly pressed top layer on the secret layer.

8. Mark the design on the top layer, either freehand or using a template.

9. Pin just outside the design areas with safety pins to hold the sandwich together.

10. Cut out a small area of the top layer to prepare it for reverse appliqué. Clip or notch seams where necessary, and pin to secure the area for quick stitching.

11. Appliqué the prepared area of the top layer to the secret layer underneath.

12. Continue preparing and stitching until you complete the appliqué design.

13. If you have used a temporary backing, swap it now for a final backing.

14. Pin-baste the sandwich with safety pins in preparation for quilting.

15. Quilt.

16. Embellish or finish, then bind and label your quilt.

A work in progress

Reverse Appliqué with Edges Turned Under

This is where we get down to the boring but necessary details!

Cutting Through the Top Layer

You've marked your design on the top layer, so let's prepare to turn under the raw edges.

If you are working a simple outline design, the marked line on the top layer becomes your cutting line. Your stitching lines will be approximately 1/4" on either side of the marked cutting line.

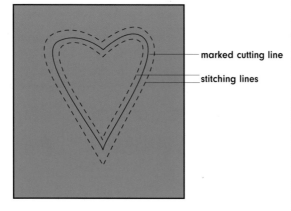

— marked cutting line
— stitching lines

If you need to cut a shape or silhouette rather than just a simple outline design, the line marked on the top layer will be your stitching line. Cut into the excess fabric of the top layer, approximately 1/4" from the marked stitching line, to create a seam allowance.

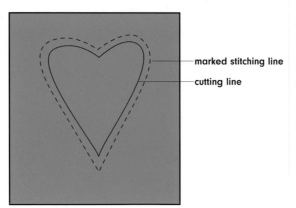

— marked stitching line
— cutting line

Corners and Points

When turning under the raw edges of the top layer, you may meet with resistance in some spots; the seam allowance won't always turn under easily. If your design is predominantly straight lines, resistance will be at the corners, and you will need to clip the seam allowance back to the stitching line to ease the tension.

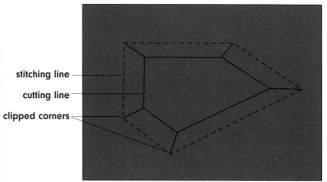

stitching line
cutting line
clipped corners

Try to keep the corner as crisp as possible. I like to manipulate the corner and finger-press it before pinning it securely. When you stitch in my primitive running-stitch style, you'll want to place the stitches so that they best secure the loose cut edges underneath.

You'll need to fold the point under when working in an outline design. If the angle is 90° or more, just fold along the first edge, and then back under with the second.

If the angle is less than 90°, you'll have to trim off some fabric before folding the edges so the seam allowance fits under the point. I like to fold under the tiniest of seams here. First I fold the fabric back to the point, and then I fold under the right and left edges. Let me tell you that this is the least pleasant maneuver of reverse appliqué! Sometimes those frayable edges want to be seen, or my fingers seem too big. I often poke with the point of my thread clippers, as they tend to offer finer control. If those points still test my patience and I'm feeling vindictive, I hold them in place with a dot of fabric glue. You can also fold, then stitch, the right side before folding and stitching the left side—the first set of stitches gives a secure area to push the fabric against.

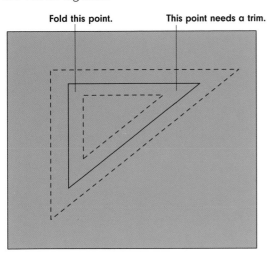

Fold this point.   **This point needs a trim.**

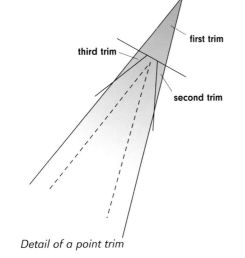

Detail of a point trim

first trim

third trim

second trim

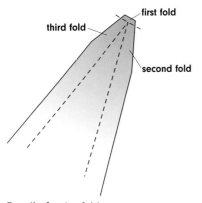

first fold

third fold

second fold

Detail of point folds

Clipping and Notching Curves

When working with curves in traditional appliqué, you need to clip and notch the seam allowance to turn it under. Reverse appliqué will give you a sweet surprise. You will generally find that there is no need for clipping or notching marked and cut circles; the bias grain and flexibility of the fabric alleviates or lessens the need. Curvy shapes that also incorporate straight edges, such as hearts and petals, usually require a bit of clipping.

So which curves do we clip and which curves do we notch? Rather than convex and concave curves—who can remember which is which?—we associate with innies and outies here (just like bellybuttons!). An innie is simple: Just clip back to the marked stitching line and turn the edges under wherever there is resistance. An outie takes two cuts to make a V, which is removed. This V cut, or notch, also goes back to the marked line.

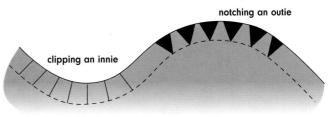

notching an outie

clipping an innie

The notches and clipping are needed at different intervals depending on the severity of the hill or valley, the innie or the outie. Minimum distance between notches and clipping is $1/4$", otherwise the seam allowance disappears! Look on the marked line and determine where the line ceases to read "straight" and starts to read "curve," then clip or notch it at that point.

This concept is illustrated best with examples—both good and bad.

Short straight lines look like curves.   **Long lines look jagged.**

Reverse Appliqué with Raw Edges

I've never been a big fan of fusible web until now: I find it has often been used without regard to the fact that fabric loses its "touch" when backed by a layer of web.

I use fusible web with raw-edge work only, and leave just a small amount on the back of the top layer once the excess fabric has been removed. The fabric feel is normal, but I now have a stable edge to stitch. Fusible web also makes transferring and preparing for appliqué a simple and accurate process; I can cut the top layer excess with a craft blade, which is a boon for intricate designs. Fusible web also gives body to the edges that will be hand or machine appliquéd, so pins and stitches don't fray the raw edges. The major limitation of this technique is that your appliqué stitches must be hardy (meaning securely machine stitched), or the quilt must remain in the decorative/wall quilt category. The kids will need other quilts to cuddle up in!

Let me take you through the preparation process.

1. Draw your design to scale. This drawing becomes your "cartoon."

2. Lay your cartoon **face down** on a lightbox. Cover the design area with a piece of fusible web, paper side up. Use a pencil to carefully trace the drawing onto the fusible web. If your design is large, consider working on it one section at a time.

If you don't have a lightbox, lay your cartoon on the table, face up, and cover the design area with a piece of fusible web, paper side down. Trace the design very carefully with a felt-tipped pen.

3. Use paper scissors to cut 1/2" to 1" from the marked design lines as shown. You'll keep this area of web (from the design line to the cut line) on the back of the top layer after you've ironed on the web and cut out the excess. This creates a non-fray edge.

design line

edge of fusible web

If you are working with lots of separate shapes, such as for the *Kids' Art Project* on page 58, leave a trail of "bridges" from shape to shape to keep the design together.

4. Position the web, paper-side up, on the back of your top layer. Press.

5. Using a craft blade and mat, cut on the marked design lines, removing the unnecessary shapes, the excess.

6. Remove the paper backing from the web.

7. Place the top layer in position, web-side down, on the secret layer and batting. Press again and you are ready to stitch.

Quilt-As-You-Go

My method of preparing reverse appliqué with batting as the base makes working on small sections especially easy. It is then simple to join these sections using one of the many quilt-as-you-go techniques. Here is a glimpse of my current favorite version, using my floating-sashing idea.

Quilt-As-You-Go with Sashing

1. Cut the four layers of the sandwich: the backing, batting, secret layer, and top layer. Cut all layers the same size; that is, about 1" larger than the final measurement on each side. This allows for take-up as you stitch.

2. Layer the sandwich, then prepare and execute the reverse appliqué of your choice.

3. Quilt the sandwich densely, making sure the stitches go right to the edge.

4. Trim the blocks to finished size. The top can still finish a little smaller than expected, so if size is critical, allow a tiny bit extra for take-up.

5. Stitch the blocks into pairs, then rows; stitch the rows together. To do this, butt the edges of the blocks against each other, and use a wide zigzag stitch and a walking foot to lessen the drag. I use masking tape instead of pins to hold the blocks together, and peel it off as it approaches the presser foot.

Use masking tape instead of pins.

6. Prepare a sashing to cover the zigzag on the back. I cut strips double the needed width and join them end-to-end to make the required length. Iron them, wrong sides together, with the raw edges meeting at the back. Working one at a time, place and pin the strips onto the back of the quilt to cover the zigzag. Try to keep the start and the finish of each strip either covered by another strip or extended out to the edge so it will be covered by the binding. Topstitch close to the edge on each side using a walking foot.

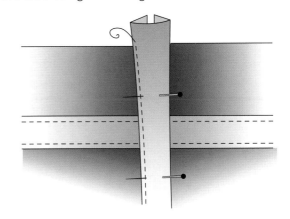

7. Cover the stitching on the front with a floating sashing as described on pages 20–21.

Floating Borders or Sashing

I rarely know how I'll border a quilt when I start the project, so I was thrilled to hit on this way of finishing my reverse-appliqué works. The idea of a floating sashing or border came about from wanting to extend the *Daisy Project* on page 53. Simply put, we make the border separately as a hollow frame, then appliqué it in position onto the quilt top. First I'll explain the process of creating a single border, then extend the idea to a sashing that you may adapt to many projects.

Floating Border

Complete your appliqué image as usual before starting on the border. The framed space may be an open secret layer or a reverse-appliqué image with a reverse-appliqué edge as on my *Daisy Project* on page 53. I can't give you specific measurements here as each application will be different. I offer just the process.

1. Mark the area on the top layer to be covered by the floating border. You may like to do this with a chalk wheel. You may prefer to measure the area with a ruler. Or, you may choose to do as I do, and simply lay the border fabric over the top layer and work by eye.

2. Before you cut the four border strips to size, you need to make allowance for the seams. I mark the finished lengths with a chalk wheel, add a 1/4" seam allowance on each end, then cut the border strips to this measurement. There is no need to add a seam allowance to the ends of the top and bottom border strips. Add at least a 1/2" seam allowance to the width of the strips.

3. Stitch the four strips together. Press.

4. Lay the floating border on your project. You may want to trim and shape the inner border edge in some areas to expose more of your secret layer or to make a curved-edge. You may be happy to merely turn the seam allowance under before pinning and reverse appliquéing. The border can be made of one fabric or scrap pieced.

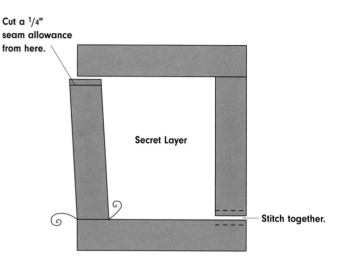

Cut a 1/4" seam allowance from here.

Secret Layer

Stitch together.

Floating Sashing

With the freeform, "crooked" way I choose to work, I use traditional straight sashings less and less. This may change with my development of the "floating sashing."

Floating sashing is similar to the floating border, with two exceptions. I like to cut the sashings on the bias, and I like to use "stops" or corner pieces for a more interesting and balanced framing effect. Cutting the sashings on the bias serves two purposes. Bias allows the length of the pieces to be cut with less accuracy, as they stretch nicely. It also allows for the appliqué edges to be manipulated in beautifully curvy lines. My *Baltimore Quilt Project* on page 67 shows off this technique to great effect.

Here's the process in a nutshell:

1. Mark the area on the top layer to be covered with a chalk wheel or by measuring it with a ruler. Or, if you prefer, simply lay the sashing fabric on the quilt top and work by eye with a little help from a tape measure.

2. Before you cut the sashings to size you need to make allowance for the bias. Since the bias sashings will stretch along the length, cut them the finished size; do not add seam allowances. Allow at least 1/2" across the width on each side of the sashing strip as a turn-under allowance.

3. Cut the stops or corner squares to the desired size, adding the usual 1/4" seam allowance.

4. Stitch the sashings and stops together to make a hollow frame. This feels like a really odd process, and you must be careful not to twist the sashings. Press the seams as you go.

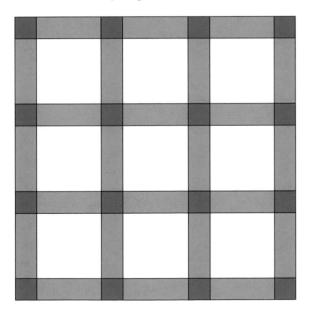

5. Lay the floating sashing on your project. Be prepared to massage the grain to get each sashing in position. I secure the perimeter edges first, pinning, then stay-stitching before I manipulate the inner pieces

to cover the seams. Turn under the raw edges before pinning and reverse appliquéing, accentuating the lack of straight lines, please!

Machine Quilting

You will see many examples of my machine quilting in this book. My method for machine quilting is a little different from the norm, as I rarely quilt in continuous lines. I prefer to quilt individual motifs repeatedly, with lots of stopping and starting. I like dense quilting, too. It holds the fabric beautifully flat.

I choose my thread colors to match the fabric being quilted. If in doubt, I choose a darker thread as it will be less visible. I use a general-purpose polyester thread for strength and because it offers a greater array of colors.

Here's how I quilted all the samples in this book. I use basically the same process to approach larger pieces.

1. Prepare the sandwich by carefully securing the layers. Use small safety pins to hold any large areas. If I plan to quilt a line around a design or shape, I form a pin-free channel for the presser foot.

2. Stitch in-the-ditch around the focal point of the piece. This stabilizes the focal point and adds a certain clarity. I usually do this quilting free-motion with the help of a quilting foot.

3. For individual quilting designs, I start and stop the stitching with a few very tiny stitches or tiny backstitches. I work one motif, starting and stopping with those tiny stitches, then jump or pull the thread to the start of the next motif. When a large area is quilted, I clip the jump threads from the front before clipping the thread from the back. I don't aim to make every motif perfect, but I try to make them fit well in the space.

Binding

I like my quilt binding to be small and tight. I find that large bindings tend to dominate the work, and—because they are rarely batting-filled—are generally too loose for my liking. Some bindings are best made from one fabric; others look great if made from an assortment.

Here's how to do it the way I do.

1. Cut enough 2"-wide strips to go around the entire quilt.

2. Turn each strip face up, and—aiming the cut to the right—cut both ends at a 45° angle.

3. Place the strips right sides together, and join them with a ¼" seam. Press the seams open.

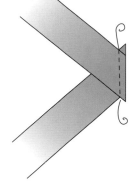

4. Press under a ¼"-wide hem at the starting angled edge. Fold the continuous binding strip in half along the length, wrong sides together, and press.

5. Starting with the turned-under edge, pin the binding to the quilt. Begin about one-third of the way across the bottom edge of the quilt, and work in a clockwise direction. Pin the binding to the quilt, making sure to line up the raw edges of the binding with the raw edges of the quilt top. Pin at 2" intervals, also making sure that the quilt is lying flat and true. Place the last pin ¼" from the first corner.

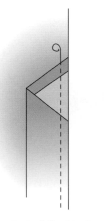

The start of the binding; the end will be tucked in here.

6. Use a walking foot to stitch from the start of the binding, using a ¼"-wide seam. Stop with a backstitch at the pin closest to the corner. Remove the quilt from the machine.

7. Lay the quilt on a table and pull the binding back at the corner to form a 45° angle. Place a pin along the outer raw edge of the binding, holding the binding in place. Pull the binding back so that it runs along the next edge.

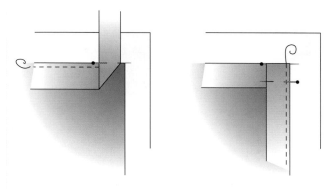

8. Proceed to pin and sew each side and miter each corner in the same manner until you are back to the bottom edge on which you started.

9. Trim the finishing end of the binding at an echoing 45° angle so that it fits snugly into the binding's starting point. Pin and stitch to complete the binding.

10. Trim the extra batting and backing so it is even with the raw edges of the binding.

11. Fold the binding to the back and pin in place.

12. Hand stitch the fold of the binding to the stitching you have just completed, folding and tucking at each corner to echo the miter on the front. I find it best to stitch in a clockwise direction to form a neater miter.

CHAPTER 3

Design

or mapping the territory

One of the exciting things about reverse appliqué is that lovely shapes, in particular curved ones, can be stitched with comparative ease. When you cut through the top layer and turn back the raw edges (perhaps after a little judicious clipping), the action of pushing back against the weave creates a fluid shape not so easily achieved with traditional appliqué.

Many styles of design are possible; the art is in matching the fabrics and techniques to achieve your vision. Let me remind you again that my style is loose and free, a little crooked and a little primitive. If you want perfect symmetry and straight lines, I give you permission to get out your rulers and compasses, but I will focus on how to achieve looks similar to mine.

Project Size

You can plan to work on a project in any size, but it is important that you *think* about the weight of materials. You'll be working with at least four layers—backing, batting, secret layer, and top—and you don't want your quilt too heavy to slumber under or pulling the plaster off the wall.

In addition to the weight of the materials, *think* about your comfort and your methods of working. If your project is large and will be executed in one piece, you will need an appropriate workspace. You may prefer projects that are smaller, more portable, and easier to work on during "waiting times." Or, you might *think* about breaking up the design. Small pieces or blocks can be joined together successfully in quilt-as-you-go methods. We look at one on page 67.

Think, too, about other ways of applying and working your design in a portable style. Working in a faux-trapunto style, we can break up the design into small sections, which can be worked on separately. See pages 50–51 for a look at my two funky trapunto versions.

Design Size

The same design can be interpreted in different ways. I've used a simple daisy motif to illustrate this.

Your design may cover the top entirely.

Your design may be used to enhance a smaller, specific area. This alternative is particularly effective if the top is pieced, embellished, or has other interesting features.

The design may be very busy,

or quite simple and sparse.

These few simple design devices should get you thinking "sideways," particularly if you are not happy with your initial drawing. They also show how you can add interest to even the simplest of images.

Theme

Choose any theme, but—for your first project especially
—consider working a simple design with simple shapes.

I've used similar images in the next chapters so you
can see how effective simple shapes can be.

Some of the following words and phrases may conjure
lovely images and jumpstart your imagination:

*names/initials/quotes
*flowers/vases/posies
*fishes/fish bowls/fishing boats
*abstract/free-form shapes/abstract overall patterns
*paper-cut designs/silhouettes/silhouette rows
*your family tree (with leaves revealing a photo)
    /individual family names/fabric from your family
*items/clothing on a clothesline/domestic objects
*nursery rhymes

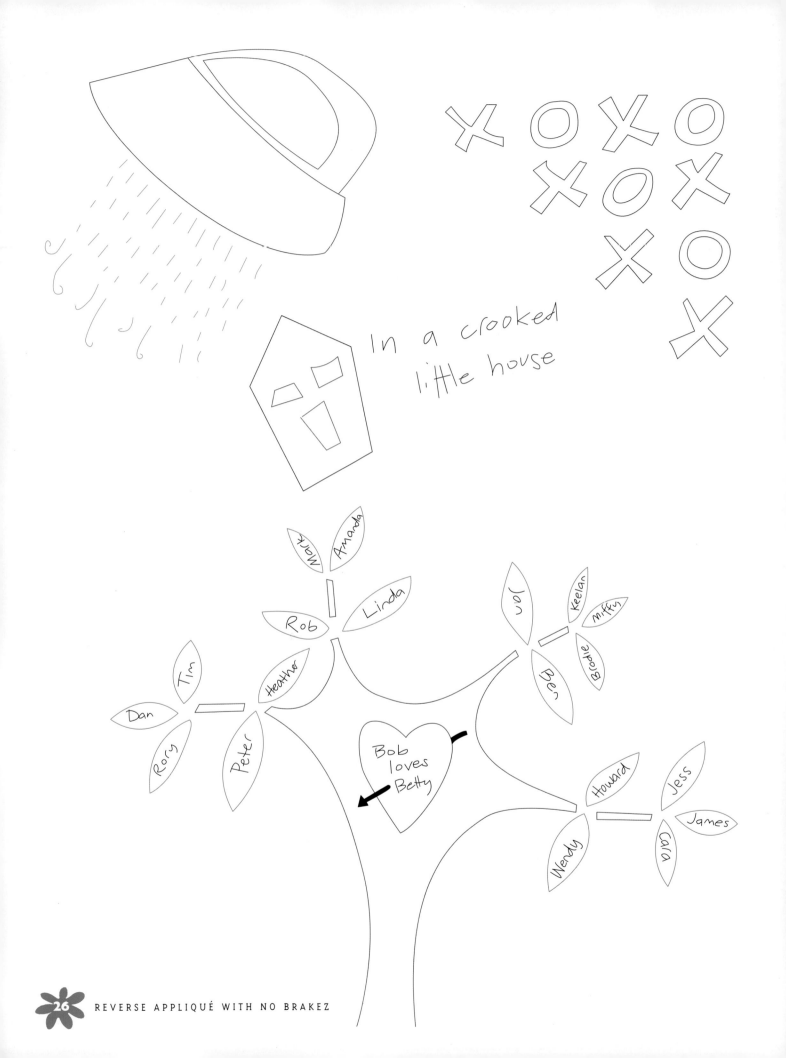

In a crooked little house

Adapting Traditional Appliqué Designs

If you love the look of traditional appliqué, particularly in the Baltimore style, you can draw—freehand, of course—the major outline of these blocks and let the secret layer fill in the color and detail. Delicious! There are plenty of excellent books, both contemporary how-to books and those showing historical quilts, to refer to for inspiration. Of course, you will then want to make my *Baltimore Quilt Project* on page 67.

Text

This is **the** method to easily incorporate text—be it your name, a quote, or your favorite saying. You can use text as the major design component or use it to add to or demystify the general design. Use any writing style: Spread it over the quilt top, place it around the edges as a border, or fling words between shapes. You are no longer bound to straight lines! See the *Twinkle, Twinkle Project* on page 65 for a preview.

Drawing the Design

First I like to do a simple thumbnail sketch on paper to capture the image. If I am working small, I then draw freehand directly on the prepared top layer with a chalk wheel or silver pencil. Done confidently, this tends to give a natural look. The chalk wheel is great for rough outlines, while the silver pencil gives a more solid line; both markers can disappear quickly, so I prefer to work in small sections. I mark and work on the major area first, and have the freedom to adapt the design by reducing, enlarging, and editing it if necessary. For example, all of the hearts and fishes in Chapters Four and Five (pages 29–41) were marked this way.

If I am working on a large scale, on an intricate piece, or on one that must be reproduced perfectly, I like to draw my design to scale on paper first so I am assured that it is balanced. I call this full-scale drawing a cartoon (see page 18), which I then use to transfer the images.

Transferring the Design

On large, intricate, or important pieces, after I have drawn my design to scale, I cut out the "holes"—the excess areas of the top layer that will be removed—so the drawing or cartoon can be used as a stencil. To keep my design intention clear, I shade or color these areas with a thick felt-tipped marker. The "holes" represent the areas that become visible in the secret layer.

Shaded areas represent the "holes."

Bridges

If the design has continuous outlined areas, be sure to leave connecting "bridges" in your work so the cartoon—and ultimately your fabric image—doesn't fall apart. There is no need to transfer the bridges to the top layer when you transfer the design.

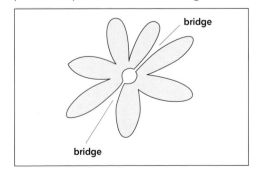

A good time to assess whether your design reveals the perfect amount of secret layer is after you've cut out the holes from the template. You may need to cut out more of the top layer to make the secret layer's presence felt. Simply audition the cartoon/template over the secret layer to have a sneak preview.

If your design is small and/or you expect you might like to repeat it in this project or another, consider transferring your design to template plastic or cardboard.

Different Styles from One Drawing

Even after you've rendered your design as a full-scale line drawing, you still have choices to make. These lines can be interpreted in different ways. Let's take the example of a simple fish being worked with raw edges.

The image can be cut on the line with the center removed.

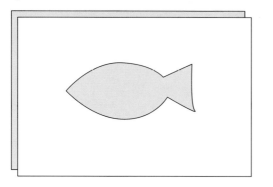

It can be cut on both sides of the line with the center of the fish left intact.

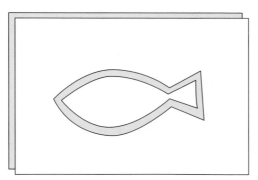

It can be detailed further to include scales and an eye.

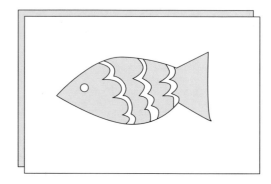

Border Design

One interesting feature of reverse appliqué is that you can plan the border as an integral part of the design right from the start. Unlike traditional quiltmaking, reverse appliqué doesn't require a straight border and binding, so you can dream up a wonderfully wobbly or intricate frame for your project. The sample below illustrates a good example. It may never be finished; it's almost interesting enough as it is!

CHAPTER 4
The Secret Layer

packing the underwear

The secret layer is as its name implies: It is hidden away. It makes its surprise appearance only when the top layer is cut, creating the design by exposing the contrast of what lies beneath.

What the secret layer looks like, how simple or complex its construction, and the materials from which it is made are unlimited. You can be focused and serious about this layer, or you can have some serious fun!

Let's look at some secret-layer choices in detail to help your ideas evolve.

Fabrics

As you travel along your reversing journey, you are more than welcome to go to town! Fabric choices include:

Quilt-weight cottons: They come in a great variety of color and pattern, are washable, and easy to use. Unless otherwise stated, my examples in this book are made from cotton. I use both yardage and scraps.

All sorts of other fabrics work well, too: silks, satins, synthetics, taffetas, wools, flannels, and sheers. These fabrics may be recycled scraps, precious pieces, or previously uncut yardage.

Fabric color is an important consideration. Generally you'll want contrast between the secret layer and the top layer. A sharply defined, high-contrast appearance is stunning, but a wavering contrast of prints or multi-colored mixes may be more appropriate to your design. Choose one color, choose an ordered palette, or surprise yourself with a mad mix.

Number of Layers

The secret layer can be the quickest and easiest layer, or the slowest to construct and most complex. Use one layer or, as in a mola version, use many.

Multiple layers offer you the option of exposing each layer methodically and consistently, or working freely to expose variations in proportion. You can expose each layer to the same degree throughout or keep some layers hidden in different areas.

♥ Solid Layer

Let's start simple and look at a single solid layer—the perfect choice if you want a crisp and clear no-nonsense look...

♥ Wild Prints

...or, if you prefer, you can use your wildest print to show snippets of unexpected color.

♥ Multiple Layers

You can extend a simple design by working with multiple layers in "even-ish" amounts to give an echo effect...

...or work again with multiples—this time to create a design within a design.

The last two examples feature three secret layers of solid fabrics, but you could easily substitute print fabrics to change the look yet again.

Pieced Layers

I love the surprises possible with pieced layers, and I really love constructing them! Often they are almost too interesting to hide. There are unlimited ways to piece layers, and I'll start you with just a few to get your brain ticking. You'll want the piecing to enhance your appliqué design, not detract from it, so you'll need to consider a few things before you begin.

Think about the size of the fabric pieces in relation to the complexity or size of your overall design.

Think about the contrast of colors, both within the secret layer and against the top layer. A highly mixed secret layer can lessen the clarity of the design—or may make a very simple design much more interesting.

Think about the clarity of the pieced design. Should it remain recognizable when the appliqué is complete, or is that to be your special secret?

By the way, don't worry about having lots of seams in this layer; cotton batting absorbs them beautifully!

Playing with Scraps

Let's start by using scraps. In this example, I have randomly pieced small multicolored scraps. (What a great way to use them!) Some pieces were square-ish, while others needed to be cut down to size. I also used triangular pieces. I simply stitched the pieces in pairs, keeping them rough, then stitched the pairs together, adding singles where needed. When the rows or columns reached the required length, I trimmed the edges to "straighten" and joined one row to the next.

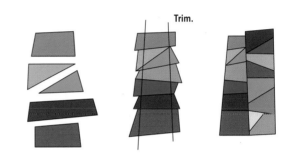

Trim.

To create a more unified scrappy secret layer, work with scraps of just one color.

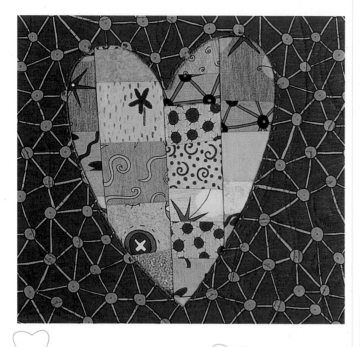

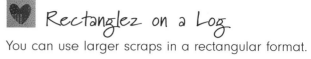

Rectanglez on a Log

You can use larger scraps in a rectangular format. Here, I've used scraps of various sizes, joining rectanglez to rectanglez and building in a bit of a Log Cabin style. This is much quicker than piecing tiny scraps, and the results are still very visually exciting. Once again, I stitch rough pieces, then trim before joining sections.

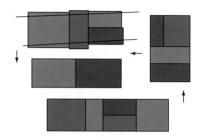

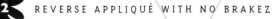

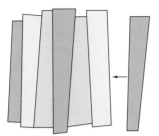 ## Tapered Strips in One Direction

You can raid the scrap basket—or cut yardage—and piece tapered strips either vertically or horizontally to create another variation on the secret layer. In the photo below, the strips taper between 1" to $1\frac{1}{2}$" over a 14" length. Stitch the strips together, alternating the taper.

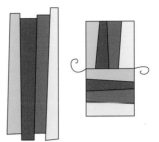 ## Tapered Strips in All Directions

How about cutting strips, making them into blocks, and then joining the blocks together? Here I cut blocks (roughly 3" square) from fabric made of tapered strips as described in the previous example. For added variety, I set the blocks in alternating directions.

Squarez in a Grid

You can use this method to enhance a regular grid as well. Here I've pieced Nine-Patchez in my cut-loose style, using two fabrics in very similar colors to make an elegant, slightly medieval-looking heart. I started out with 5"-ish squares, stacked, sliced, switched, and stitched, and then trimmed them back to perfect 3½" squares.

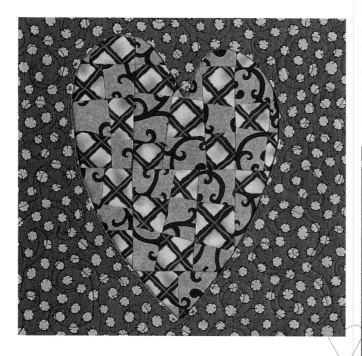

Colorwash Fun

If you are a colorwash aficionado, you can use your leftover squares for a subtle, ordered-color, playful effect. Imagine a sunset design with the colors blending behind....

I've taken the colorwash idea a step further in the next example. I cut pairs of 3½" squares in gradated colors, lined them up in that gradation, paired them with both their forward and backward neighbors, and then stacked, sliced, switched, and stitched them as cut-loose Four-Patchez blocks. Finally, I trimmed them to 2½" squares, and then stitched them together in gradated order.

Stack, Slice, Switch

For another fun exercise, stack a few large squares, slice them, switch the fabrics, and stitch them back together. Of course my slices are skewed! I cut four 8" squares and continually stacked, sliced, switched, and stitched them until the pieces fit my heart's desire.

This is a surprise from start to finish, and a great way to get a scrappy look from just a few fabrics.

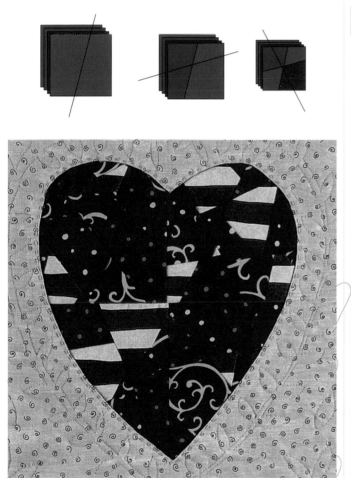

Stitching Directly on the Batting

Here's a different approach. It involves working directly on the batting: stitching fabric, and adding embroidery, embellishments, and other enhancements until the secret layer forms a luscious secondary design peeking through the top layer. Lots of textile-enhancement techniques are easy to execute; once again, I'll suggest just a few.

Contemporary Crazy

Try freely stitching raw-edge scraps straight onto the batting, in a contemporary crazy-pieced style. My example uses tiny pieces of cottons, with free-motion stitching to hold them in place. I ironed a layer of fusible web to the batting first to make application easy. After removing the paper from the web, I arranged the scraps in finished position and carefully pressed them to hold for stitching.

Fancy and Crazy

Here's an even fancier version, using the same type of raw-edge scraps, but this time using decorative stitches to sew them straight onto the batting, reminiscent of Victorian crazy piecing. This technique creates a very sturdy piece. Once again, I used a layer of fusible web under my scraps. My stitches are freely stitched, but programmed machine stitches would be just as nice. Decorative threads would be yummy, too!

Colorful Solids

You can stitch or quilt a solid piece of fabric with intricate/colorful lines of random or planned stitching to create your secret layer. What could be nicer than this underquilt of stars? Perhaps a love letter quilted all over your secret layer, revealing only the best bits?

Embellishers' Delight

Embellishers will enjoy enhancing this layer with braids and ribbons. My example is rather simple, but I know many of you will delight in taking this idea further.

The Secret in Full?

Up until this point, we've assumed that the secret layer will completely cover the batting. This is how I usually like to work so I can modify my design at any stage and expose more color if necessary, perhaps on a border. This approach also makes for consistent thickness throughout and even coloration if the top layer is in any way transparent.

Perhaps, however, you prefer just a small area revealed, or you'd rather not spend time or precious fabric on an area that won't be seen. In this case, prepare your cartoon as a template first and use it as a guide to pin or tack the partial secret layer in position on the batting. I used this method in both the *Twinkle, Twinkle Project* (see page 64) and the *Kids' Art Project* (see page 58).

You might also consider the option of planning fabric placement to enhance your chosen design (for example, leaf areas can be green and flower areas yellow). Of course, you can do this in a full secret layer, too. Once again, you will need to prepare your cartoon as a template.

CHAPTER 5

The Top Layer

or choosing the overcoat

The top layer usually creates the frame for a wonderful secret layer. Rather than compete, its role is to enhance the secret layer: no excuse to be boring or conservative here!

Fabric Color

Usually you'll want contrast between the top and secret layers. Black is an obvious color choice for the top layer. It's the one I started reversing with. It creates a beautiful contrast, and makes the fabrics in the secret layer glow.

White or pale colors are a bit more difficult—unless the fabric is very opaque. Otherwise, the colors of the secret layer show (or "shadow") through, and the results may not be quite what you had planned. In the example shown here, the print tends to diffuse the hints of color coming through. The black stitching of the reverse appliqué also helps to shift the focal point away from shadows.

Other color choices can be wonderful, too. I have included examples of different looks to expand your possibilities, though I do admit they are all based on brights!

Printed Fabric

Small dots, stripes, textures, tone-on-tones, or repeat patterns work as well as, or even better than, solids as they offer a bit more visual interest and may provide a tie-in with the secret layer.

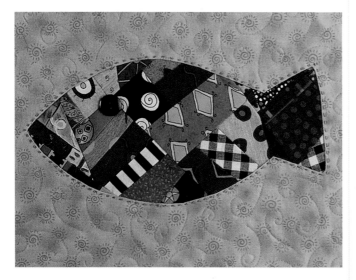

Try something wild on top with perhaps the plainest of dark fabrics as your secret layer (that's reversing twice over!). Here I have kept the fish as an outline to accentuate the effect of the strong contrast. If you were using text in your design a similar effect would work well.

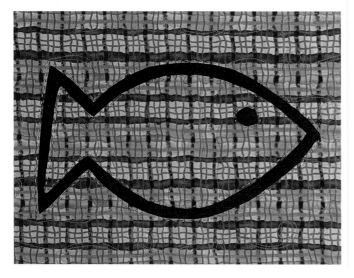

Fabric Types

Most of the examples here have been made with quilt-weight cottons, same as for the secret layer. Cottons work well; they are readily available, are the perfect weight, are easy to cut through and turn under, and come in an infinite range of colors and patterns.

I have also been known to use linen and synthetics, velvet, flannels, wools, and sheers! The results, and the stitching techniques needed to achieve them, may be somewhat different, but that is part of the fun.

Here are three examples that use varied fabrics.

Flannel

Wool

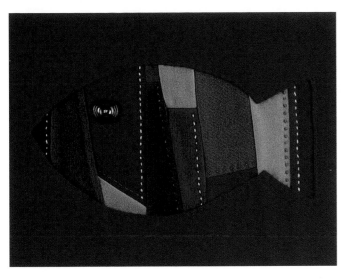

Sheer Chiffon

Pieced Fabric

Just as you can piece the secret layer in a myriad of ways, you can also piece the top layer. Generally, I advise that you keep the piecing rather simple and sparse, or it may be difficult to cut through and appliqué. Think of a pieced top layer as a design device, a way to extend your design—perhaps to add more definition, more color, more pattern, or even a border.

Distinct Design Areas

What if you'd like to create a landscape or a seascape? Here I've also worked the secret layer in three distinct color and design areas to define the images.

Still Life

You can move the same theory and process indoors to create a still life. This example shows a tablescape that once again includes two fabrics in the top layer. The secret layer includes two layers, and neither layer extends to the edge of the piece!

Other Piecing Options

There are other options as well. You could divide the top into squarez, or irregular pieces.

You could also divide the top into irregular pieces.

You might even piece simple, large bands of fabrics to use as a design device.

Pieced Blocks

If you start thinking about pieced blocks, you can take the technique so much further. I love my group of Sawtooth Stars with the simple circle design in each center and block corner. Does it matter that the stars are not fish?

Intricate Designs

When the top layer features an intricate design with lots of close cutting, I like to apply fusible web to the back and keep the edges raw. For example, I've used just a single line of machine stitching to hold and define this fish design. This method is also very effective for different styles and methods of stitching. I'll show you other examples in the next chapter.

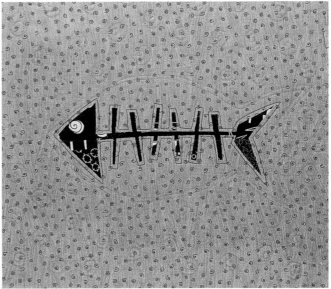

CHAPTER 6

Reverse Appliqué

or off and racing in reverse

You've covered the batting with a secret layer, and you've placed the top layer and marked your design. The next step is the actual appliqué—the main feature, the star of the show.

Here's a brief review of the limitless variations possible, with the first major choice being whether to reverse appliqué by hand or machine.

Reversing by Hand

Perhaps the best way to explore the options is for me to show you some examples.

My first choice, remember, is to turn the raw edges under and, using six strands of embroidery floss in the same color as the top layer, to execute a sweet and rather primitive running stitch. How could I limit you, though, to just one look?

Traditional Appliqué

You could use the traditional appliqué technique of turned-under edges and invisible stitches. This familiar approach does have its place if you want something a bit more elegant and perhaps with pointier points!

Buttonhole Stitch

Here I have left the edges raw and used fusible web to secure them. The stitch gives a lovely clean line on the raw edge. Have a look at the difference thread color makes here; pulling the color out of the stalk makes it prickly, while using the background color on the petals defines the shape. I used only one strand of embroidery floss for a delicate treatment.

Stab Stitch

This one has great potential! Again, I've used different colors of thread to create prickly stalks and feather-edged petals. This time I turned the raw edges under and the edge looks a little more solid.

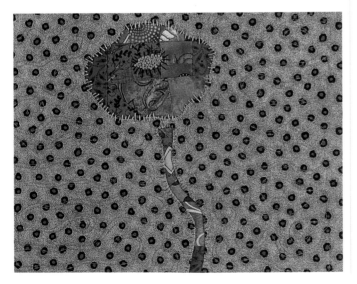

 ## Cross Stitch

This is another pleasurable and solid stitch. Here I've used not only different colors of thread, but different-sized stitches in a varied number of strands to keep the thread and stitch in proportion. I've used one strand for the stalk, two for the leaves, and three strands for the flower. I turned the raw edges under, and just couldn't resist quilting this with crosses, too!

Feather and Cretan Stitch

I love the feather stitch. It isn't appropriate everywhere, but is very effective here. It covers and almost knits the secret and top layers together. In this example, I used Cretan stitch for the stalk, as the feather stitch didn't have a tough enough look. I stitched both areas with a single strand and left the edges of the fabrics raw.

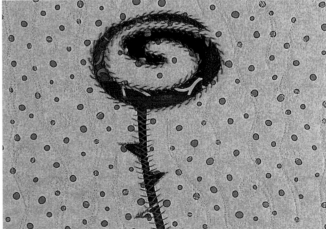

Threads

Stitches can be a "shameless" feature, or they may try to take a back seat to the design. The effect depends not only on size and type of the stitch, but also on the choice and color of thread.

You can choose threads of many different fibers, weights, and styles, but they must be easy to stitch with! If you can't stitch with the thread, consider couching it.

These next three examples all have turned-under edges.

 ## Subtlety in Cotton

The first sample shows a small running stitch in quilting cotton—subtle, but easy to execute.

 ## Variegated Embroidery

The next sample shows a medium-sized running stitch in embroidery floss—this one a variegated type.

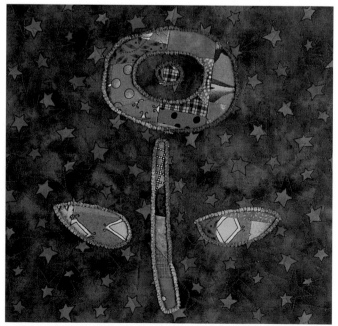 ## Couched Chenille

Finally, I've used a gorgeous variegated chenille thread, held against the turned edge by a couching stitch worked in a fine cotton. I loved doing this, and I love the effect.

Reversing by Machine

Machine work tends to have a flatter, less dimensional look, but it is also quicker, and opens our eyes to completely different styles.

You can turn under the raw edges if you like, and stitch close to the edge, but I prefer to utilize the raw edges, covering or holding them in various ways, with various stitches. All of the following examples are raw edged, and all but the last use fusible web to stabilize the edges.

 ### Freehand and Straight

The first simple example uses freehand straight stitches. I dropped the feed dogs to take control of the stitch length, width, and direction. A single line in a green thread slightly darker than the top layer is enough to accentuate and hold the shape. Of course, this method is not ideal for a child's bed, but would be great for a quilt meant for the wall.

The next three examples are of similar decorative bent. All are executed freehand. I tried to accentuate their "personality" and petal shapes by stitching in different styles; this required contrasting threads.

Scribbly

The first shows my scribbly style: tiny insecure stitches with the lines held by tight knots on both the flower and along the stem. The quilting reiterates the nervous and delicate quality of the flower.

Stitched Layers

Example number two is the star of the show: strong, but subtle. I used repeated layers of stitching in a variety of fine rayon threads, and overpowered the straight cut edges with wavy stitches.

This copious amount of stitching pulls in the quilt sandwich and ruffles the fabric. To overcome this, quilt the background at a similarly intense level.

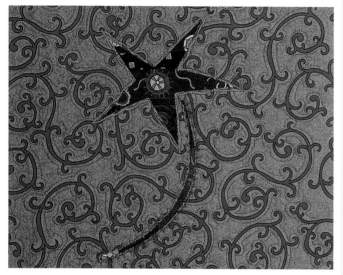

My final freehand-stitched example is a sunflower, again of simple design. This time I used two lines of stitching, crossing them over each other almost haphazardly rather than just echoing them. The simple crosses in the center are easy to do, and add a great texture.

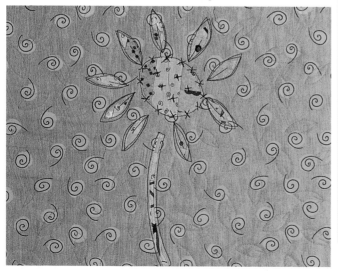

Decorative Stitches

You can have just as much fun if you prefer to use the set stitches on your sewing machine. This is not an area I had explored before—I am happy being free!—but I was very pleased with my first results.

All but the most basic of sewing machines offer decorative stitches. I suggest you look to your machine's manual for the gory details of which knobs to fiddle with. I've included the result of my playing to inspire you.

Starting with a small satin stitch on the stalk and leaves—not my favorite stitch I must admit—I progressed to a triangular version on the petals to give my flower attitude.

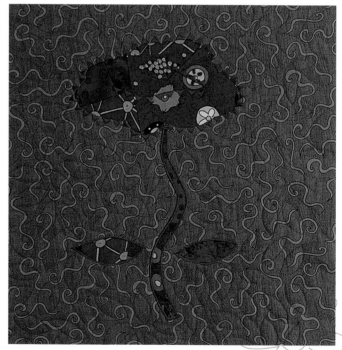

Next are two machine-stitched buttonhole stitches: sturdy, pleasant to look at, and pretty easy to do despite all the pointy bits. I love how buttonhole stitch looks with reverse appliqué. On the petals, it sits on the reverse side of the design, but on the center of the flower, which is technically "proper" appliqué, it sits as is "normal."

This next example features a different array of stitches —all to remain nameless. These stitches add to the design and are not especially difficult to execute: just the corners and pointy bits are tiresome. The result is another sturdy version for wrapping up the kids!

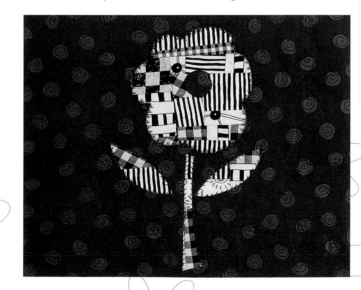

 Stitching, Then Cutting

The last bit of reverse appliqué I have to offer is a bit different. The idea here is to stitch your design, *then* cut out areas of your choice to expose the secret layer. I've used repeated rounds of small freehand machine stitches to create my outline, and have used my clippers to cut right to the edge of this very secure stitching. I've left a leaf uncut to show you the "before" effect. With lots of rounds of stitching, I needed to quilt the background profusely too.

Of course different threads and stitches can change the look considerably.

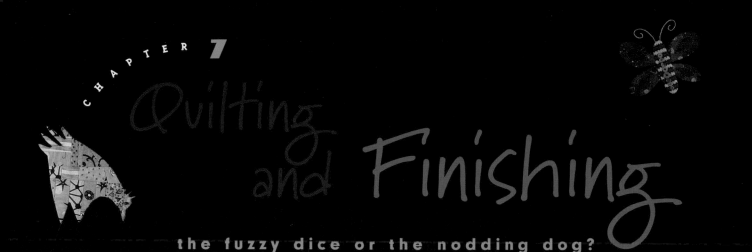

You will have made many choices along the way as your work has progressed. Now you can tie the design together, and add that final, delightful touch. How you choose to quilt and finish your piece should reflect and enhance what you've done so far. Take the time and due care to complete your vision.

Threads

Once again it's a case of decisions, decisions, decisions! Your favorite thread shop will offer plenty of options including cottons, silks, rayons, and synthetics in unlimited weights, colors, plies, and styles to suit hand or machine quilting. Choose threads to enhance quietly or add the finishing fireworks.

Hand Quilting

The options continue: In addition to thread (type, weight, color, etc.), you'll need to make choices about stitches and proportion. Looking at my samples will give you a few ideas. You may choose to downplay the quilting, or to feature it.

Consider using the same thread for the quilting as you used for the appliqué. For example, if you have used embroidery floss for the hand appliqué, it would be logical to follow by quilting with the same type of thread.

Echo Stitching

Echo stitching, which repeats the outline of the shape, works well to reiterate and accentuate a simple design. In the following example, I continued with the same colored embroidery floss, once again using the full six strands: a simple and serene study of stargazing. Not bad for a dog lover!

Textured Stitching

Textured stitching can also be very effective. Simple stab-and-cross stitches are easy to execute, and—when worked in the same thread as the appliqué—add rather than overpower or detract. This cat is grazing on the grass, at night of course, as he is stargazing.

Tying

Your piece may only need to be tied. I love leaving the threads to hang on the front to form additional texture. This is particularly nice on flannels and wools. My final cat, with double-button eyes, not only sits among a flurry of perle cotton threads, but also sports tied, embroidery-floss whiskers!

My simple tying method is a breeze, too. Take a basic backstitch, leaving a tail at the start, then re-enter the stitch from the right, and cut off, leaving another tail at the left. It is quick and easy to execute, and impossible to pull out.

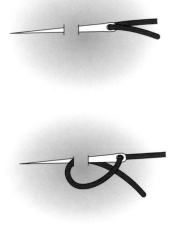

Machine Quilting

Again, try to choose a quilting motif and thread to suit your work thus far. Hide the quilting, or feature it.

Some images need only simple lines or grids: quick, easy, and no-nonsense.

Adding Text

I usually quilt freehand. I like to quilt my pieces quite intensely with lots of textures or motifs hidden by sewing thread the same color as the top layer. I particularly love designs that add to the quilt's story. I find it easy to include text as well. Text here adds to the whimsy of the dreaming dog.

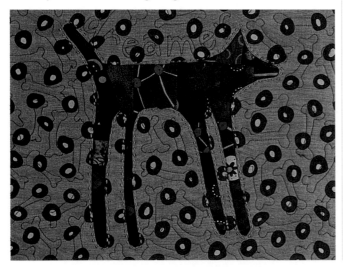

Embellishing

Is your design too plain for your crazy tastes? Is it lacking a bit of pizzazz or a focus? Take it to another realm through the world of embellishment.

Try adding buttons, beads, or appliqué on the top layer—the reverse of reverse! In this example, I've used all of these, including appliquéing organza on the wings, and appliqué over a batting base to build up the body. The antennas were couched, and the reverse appliqué was stab-stitched.

That's surely one with the lot!

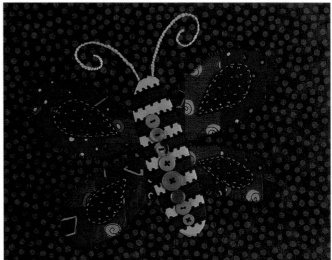

Adding Dimension/ Mock Trapunto

You may like to work in a mock-trapunto style to add a bit of bulk or presence to your focal image. I offer you two ways to work. Both involve working on small individual pieces to complete the reverse appliqué, and then trimming the batting slightly larger than the appliqué area.

With the first method the top layer is trimmed to echo the appliqué before being stitched to another sandwich.

The second method involves keeping the top layer intact, then piecing one "block" to the next. Make sure with both methods that they are securely held by quilting on completion of the re-sandwiching/piecing, particularly in the area where the first cut-down layer of batting ends.

I've trimmed the first top-layer backward-looking bunny to ¼" past the bunny-shaped batting, then clipped and turned it under the edge of the batting. I then appliquéd the prepared bunny to another batting/top-layer sandwich with an invisible appliqué stitch.

Yes, it takes time, but the extra "border" around the bunny and the extra layer does give it presence. For a finishing touch, I filled the fluffy tail with shredded batting.

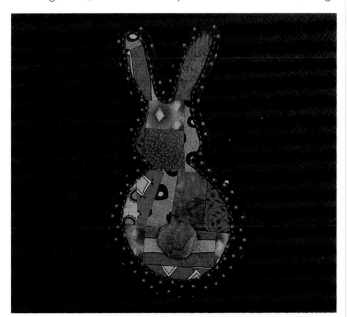

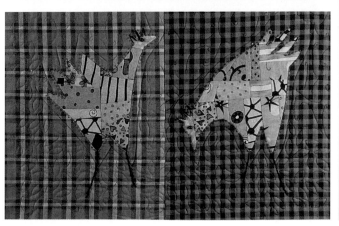

My chooks—that is, chickens—have not been left with a border like my bunny. Instead I left their top layers as they were cut initially, merely squaring each up, and pieced together to form a bigger top. Then I placed this larger, combined top over another full layer of batting and backing before I began the quilting.

Finishing the Edge

Some projects will need traditional binding. I like my bindings small and tight, so I use a 2"-wide strip folded wrong sides together. See page 22 for greater detail.

You may choose to use lots of fabric scraps to continue your mad mix, or perhaps use a fabric in the same color as your top layer so the binding blends in. You may need or prefer something quite stark to tie all the elements together. Whatever your direction, take time to make the best possible decision.

Be prepared to keep an open mind, as there are ways other than traditional binding to finish a fabric piece.

My first two reverse appliqué quilts had unusual edges. For one, I joined the edges with a running stitch, adding cross-stitch for a bit of focus.

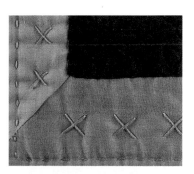

For the other, I folded and stitched the raw edge of the wide, bias-cut border to the back.

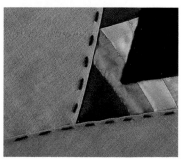

CHAPTER 8

Projects

or fresh road trips

The purpose of projects in any quilting book should be not only to get readers rushing to the sewing machine, but also to reinforce the main content of the previous chapters. I have tried to combine a diverse selection of skills and techniques in only six projects. Think of this as an introduction to the mixing and matching you may end up doing.

The projects are set up to show you what techniques we will cover, to give you insight into my decisions, and also allow room for your variations.

Consider these a collection of road maps for your continuing joyride.

DAISY PROJECT

Finished Size: 16" x 21"

Specimen Daisy by Jan Mullen, 2002

This was a teaching sample for quite a few years, a small piece I had never planned on finishing but grew to love, as did many of my students. It is a great way to start working in reverse, small and portable with a variety of techniques covered.

Design

Designed to practice innies and outies, points, and working with a template containing a bridge.

Thumbnail sketch

Fabrics and Threads

Secret layer: assorted small yellow scraps

Top layer, red print: Cut 12" x 18".

Floating border: assorted small red scraps

Backing: Cut 18" x 23".

Batting: Cut 18" x 23".

Binding: 1/4 yard red/yellow-striped print

Appliqué thread: 1–2 skeins black embroidery floss

Stitching/quilting thread: red and yellow

The Process

1. Draw the daisy approximately 10" x 15", on paper fitting within the size of the top layer.

Cut out the holes so the cartoon can be used as a template. The center of the flower will need a bridge.

2. Cut the backing and batting.

3. Piece the secret layer. I used a variety of small yellow scraps stitched into rows, then sewed the rows together to make a new fabric to cover the batting. Lay the freshly pressed secret layer on the batting.

4. Position the top layer over the secret layer. Center it, as it will be smaller than the rest of the sandwich.

5. Mark the design on the top layer using the template and a silver pencil.

6. Pin around the design areas with safety pins to hold the sandwich together.

7. Cut out the first area to be reverse appliquéd, clipping seams where necessary. Turn under the edges and pin to secure the area for quick stitching. The stalk and the leaves are the easiest if you need to warm up!

8. Stitch the prepared appliqué area. I used 6 strands of embroidery floss and my favorite running stitch. Continue until the appliqué is complete.

9. Mark and turn under the outer edges of the top layer. Pin and appliqué using the same thread and stitch. I didn't keep my edge straight; I opted to give it a slightly rounded feel.

10. Prepare the floating border by stitching together assorted small red scraps into 4 approximately 3" x 16½" rectangles (refer to page 20 for more detail). Stitch the 4 sides together, lay them over the secret layer, and appliqué, again using the same thread and stitch.

With this edge I trimmed and pulled back the corners to accentuate and enlarge them.

11. If you have used a temporary backing, now is the time to swap it for the final one. Use safety pins to prepare the sandwich for quilting.

12. I free-motion quilted this piece in three parts. First, I stitched in-the-ditch of the daisy, stalk, leaves, and border to define them. The second area to quilt was the top layer, which I covered with daisies. Finally, I stitched a border of continuous leaves; this is about as continuous as my quilting gets!

13. I bound this daisy in the perfect single fabric: a red and yellow stripe.

KITTY PROJECT

Finished Size: 14" x 17"

K Is for Kitty by Jan Mullen, 2002

REVERSE APPLIQUÉ WITH NO BRAKEZ

K is for Kitty sitting pretty on the wall, staring at the stars. She started her life as a technical sample made merely to linger among the other animals in Chapter Seven. Determined to shine solo, she is displayed here in her complete serenity. She's a fresh young thing, this Kitty, and with simple pieced borders and embroidered details to ground her, she is a very simple project.

This project can be made from scratch, but you can, like me, enlarge a smaller sample. Simply add on some extra batting around the edges with a wide zigzag stitch, then cut border strips with a rotary cutter to equal the sides, top, and bottom. Stitch them on with a wide zigzag stitch, then you can add the top layer borders. *I'd love to do a complete alphabet set like this. P would have to be for Puppy of course!*

Design

Thumbnail sketch

Fabrics and Threads

Secret layer: assorted small black
  and white scraps
Top layer, red print: Cut to 10" x 13".
Border, assorted black print scraps:
  2½" x various lengths
Backing: Cut 16" x 19".
Batting: Cut 16" x 19".
Binding: ¼" yard black solid
Appliqué thread: 1 skein each of
  black and red embroidery floss
Stitching /quilting thread: black

The Process

1. Draw Kitty to fit the top layer, approximately 10" x 13". Cut out kitty so that the cartoon can be used as a template.

2. Cut the backing and batting.

3. Piece the secret layer. I used a variety of small black and white scraps stitched into rows, then sew the rows together to make a new fabric about 6" x 10". Lay the freshly pressed secret layer on the batting.

4. Position the top layer over the secret layer. Center them, as they will be smaller than the rest of the sandwich.

5. Mark the design on the top layer using the template and a silver pencil.

6. Pin around the design areas with safety pins to hold the sandwich together.

7. Cut out the area to be reverse appliquéd, clipping seams where necessary. Turn under the edges and pin to secure the area for quick stitching.

8. Stitch the prepared appliqué area. I used 6 strands of cotton and my favorite running stitch. Continue until the appliqué is complete.

9. If you have used a temporary backing now is the time to swap it for the final one. Use safety pins to prepare the sandwich for quilting.

10. I hand quilted Kitty in an echo style, without marking, and simply stitched in rounds about an inch apart. Quilt right to the edges of the top layer.

11. Time for the borders. I cut strips of black print fabric 2½" wide and auditioned them around the edges of the top layer, trying to create color and line balance. The sides were pieced, the top and bottom simply one fabric each.

Cut the sides 13" x 2½". Pin each to the side edges of the top layer, right sides together and raw edges aligned. Stitch/quilt in place; I used my walking foot here.

Cut the top and bottom 14" x 2½". Pin each to the top layer, right sides together and raw edges aligned. Stitch in place.

12. Using black embroidery floss, quilt around the inner and outer edges of the border to hold in place.

13. With a chalk wheel mark a simple "K" and a "fence line." Using the full 6 strands, doubled, stitch along these markings, once again in running stitch.

14. Kitty was bound in black solid fabric.

Keelan talking to the dog who is barking at the bird by Jan Mullen, 2002

Years ago I used a drawing of Miffy's and one of Brodie's as a base for a small quilt. Somehow Keelan missed out and he reminded me a while back of my omission. We picked out a great line drawing from the stack available and it's been waiting on the pin-up board ever since. Finally, over thirteen years since its creation, I've taken the time to reproduce it in fabric.

I looked to Keelan for his input in my interpretation: What was essential and what was dispensable? I had narrowed down the choice of background fabrics and he was very clear, "No grass in the sky, no stars on the ground," so I had to use both and form a horizon! Another option was to choose a fabric the color of aged paper, but we both agreed it was too boring. Other easy decisions were the sun, the bird's beak, and Keels himself. He was red, they were yellow—simple. I then had

leeway with the bird and the dog to pull the design together.

The line drawing that we worked from gave me the inspiration to couch a black line everywhere Keelan had marked. I love the effect. It keeps the images crisp and the colors clear and bright. The images had to be transferred with accuracy, so I traced the design onto fusible web so it could be cut out with my craft knife. This would give me a top layer template to audition the secret layer through and strengthen the raw-edge work.

I kept the layers big for the potential border, but in the end I felt it needed none; it would have been too contrived.

We are both thrilled with our collaboration.

Design

Taken from an original drawing and reproduced to scale.

I do not expect you to reproduce Keelan's drawing; it was only meant to inspire you to choose one of your own that has meaning to you.

Fabrics and Threads

Secret layer: assorted scraps in various colors
Top layer, blue sky: Cut 34" x 19".
Green grass: Cut 34" x 8".

Backing: Cut 34" x 26".
Batting: Cut 34" x 26".
Binding: 1/4 yard of blue star fabric
Couching thread: 1 ball black 8-ply wool
Stitching/quilting thread to match fabrics
Fusible web: Cut 2 pieces 31" x 23" each.

The Process

1. Cut the backing and batting.

2. Stitch the sky to the grass. Press.

3. Trace the image onto the paper side of one piece of fusible web using the technique described in reverse appliqué with raw edges on page 18, Steps 1 through 5.

4. Trace the image again, this time onto the second piece of fusible web. Keep both the drawing and the web paper face up. Cut around the image, giving it a frame of 1/2" to 1". Position this on your batting, fuse, and peel off the paper. The secret layer scraps are adhered to this before stitching.

5. Position the top layer over the batting. It's now time to audition lots of scraps in the "holes" to come up with a balanced mix. Take your time and be prepared to trim bits as necessary. Fuse scraps as desired.

6. Peel off the web paper from the top layer, then position it back on the secret layer. Carefully press the fabric all over to secure for stitching.

7. Pin around the design areas with safety pins to hold the sandwich together.

8. Carefully stitch around all the raw edges to secure. Keep the stitches as close to the edges as possible so they will be hidden, along with the raw edge, under the couching. I did this freehand and used thread to match the grass or the sky.

9. The next job was to quilt all areas. The fabrics within the images were held by their raw edge, then given texture or definition as needed. The sky and grass were treated as sky and grass!

10. Now for the couching. My wool was rather stretchy, which made it a bit more difficult to work with, but it was the perfect width. To start and stop I threaded it on a large needle, avoiding lumps or fraying at the front. Using black stitching thread, I freehand stitched/couched the wool over the raw edges. I constantly referred back to Keelan's drawing for the fine details.

Detail

11. A double-button eye was stitched on the dog. A few French knots with the couching thread were all that was needed for the other eyes and nostrils.

12. After adding the binding and a label the quilt was complete.

Some thoughts on working with kids' art...

*Keep the essence of the drawing, clean up and interpret if you have to, but don't pretend it is yours to change.
*Usually there is ownership involved; years later Keelan knew what he had drawn and why. He gave me permission to reproduce his drawing but not ruin his vision.

FLANNEL QUILT PROJECT

Finished Size: 60" x 72"

Warm Spotz by Jan Mullen, 2002

The inspiration for this quilt was twofold. I had been asked repeatedly by students whether reverse appliqué is sturdy and can be used on bed quilts. This project is proof of my positive response. I also had some new flannels to play with. What I came up with is a very practical bed quilt for a cold winter's night! I used three layers of flannels and cotton batting as well. The weight was only a problem when machine quilting, proving to be better than a trip to the gym!

The appliqué was a breeze, though. Rough marked circles and no clipping or notching because the wonderful bias grains did their work.

Design

Designed to have "block"-style piecing on the top layer as well as ordered strip piecing on the secret layer. I tried very hard to keep the design simple.

Fabrics and Threads

Secret layer: 24 fat quarters of flannels, predominately green

Top layer: ½ yard each of 10 flannels, predominantely blue

Backing fabric: 2¼ yards each of 2 blue flannels

Batting: Cut 64" x 76".

Binding: ½ yard black flannel

Appliqué thread: 4–5 skeins black embroidery floss

Stitching/quilting thread: blue, green, black, and red

The Process

Top layer: thirty 12" blocks
Secret layer: sixty-three 9" blocks

1. For the top layer: Cut 30 squares, each 12½". Arrange them in a 5 x 6 block setting so the color and prints are balanced. If you arrange them with the majority of the lengthwise grains vertical, as I did, it will stitch together easily with little stretch. Stitch blocks together in rows, then sew rows together, pressing as you go.

2. For the secret layer: Stack the fat quarters in groups of 4 with lengthwise grains aligned. Slice them into tapered strips along the lengthwise grain, keeping them a minimum width of 1" and a maximum width of 2½".

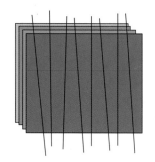

Join the strips together in sets of 8 (or to equal 9"), pressing as you go. Cut these fabrics into 9" squares; you will need 63 squares.

If any of your strip fabrics or squares is short simply add another strip in any direction (either it won't be seen or it will look quirky).

Lay out and arrange the blocks in a 7 x 9 block setting, alternating strip directions, before stitching together in rows, then sewing the rows together.

3. For the backing: Stitch the 2 pieces together along the lengthwise grain. Press.

4. Sandwich the backing, batting, secret layer, and top layer. The secret layer is sized slightly differently from the top layer but no matter, it will be held. Pin the block seams with a channel of safety pins and a few pins to hold the block centers.

5. With the walking foot, stitch the block seams in-the-ditch and around the top layer perimeter. This will hold the sandwich while the appliqué is executed.

6. Use your chalk wheel to mark a big, loose, and crooked circle within each block. Using thread clippers, cut on that line, or in a little if size is critical, and remove the "spot." For all but the first one to be stitched, pin around the edges with safety pins to hold. For the first, turn under the raw edges and pin with medium-sized pins.

7. Using six strands of embroidery floss, execute a large running stitch around the edges of the spot. Repeat for all the spots.

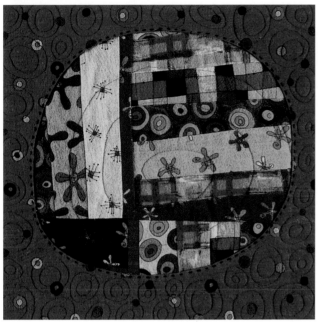

Detail

8. I free-motion quilted this piece in the secret/top layer in every block. I chose a few of my favorite motifs that blended well with the print of the fabrics. I also stitched in-the-ditch around the spot, continuing into the center with a spiral.

9. The quilt was bound in a black flannel print. Yummy and very snug.

TWINKLE, TWINKLE PROJECT

Finished Size: 15" x 17" each

Twinkle by Jan Mullen, 15" x 17", 2002

Twinkle etc. by Jan Mullen, 15" x 17", 2002

I was getting desperate to use some of my luxury fabrics in a project but it took some time to evolve. I had two chiffon scarves, one purple and one red, and while playing with them "Twinkle, twinkle" kept running through my head. I hadn't used many stars in the samples either. Could I put the whole nursery rhyme in the piece? It would have to be big and I didn't have enough fabric....

Twinkle, twinkle etc. was spread over two pieces. I can't wait to do *Baa, baa black sheep* now! (Oops, was that me thinking again?)

I haven't finished these pieces in the usual bound-and-edged manner of quilt art. These are to be stretch-mounted over a foam board.

Design

Designed to incorporate text, stitching before revealing the secret, and using some gorgeous and yummy slippery fabrics.

Thumbnail sketches

Fabrics and Threads

Lower secret layer, 1 purple and 1 red: Cut each 15" x 17".

Secret layer: assorted small red and purple scraps of yummy fabrics

Top layer, yummy red: Cut 19" x 21". Yummy purple. Cut 19" x 21".

Over-layer: a red chiffon scarf and a purple chiffon scarf

Batting: Cut 2 pieces 19" x 21" each.

Fusible web: Cut 2 pieces 15" x 17" each.

Hand-appliqué and quilting thread: one skein each of red and purple rayon embroidery floss

Machine-appliqué and quilting thread: red and purple rayon

The Process

Each piece is worked the same way with a swapping of colors between layers keeping them easy to balance.

1. Iron the fusible web to the center of the batting. Peel off the paper. Iron on the lower secret layer. This fabric is to be seen under the text and also to peek out between the scraps of the star.

2. Cut the secret-layer scraps into small rectangles. Start stitching the red ones on the red layer and the purple ones on the purple layer. I stitched them freehand, going around their edges once or twice, overlapping fabrics when I needed interest. You need to cover approximately the center third.

3. Place the top layer and over layer on each piece, the red top and over layer on the purple secret layer, and vice versa. Pin lightly around the sandwich with safety pins.

4. With a chalk wheel mark the star and the text on the top/over layer. Pin next to these lines to hold for stitching.

5. Using the same colored thread as the top layer, stitch on the star line and also around the text. I stitched a single line, but a double line or more decorative stitch could look good, too. Make sure the narrowest part of the text is no less than $1/4$".

6. Secret time. With the clippers cut the over layer $1/4$" inside the star. Then cut the top layer another $1/4$" inside that to reveal the secret layer.

7. Pin and stab-stitch over the edges of the top layer with a single strand of rayon the same color as the secret layer.

8. Very carefully expose the secret layer in the text. Keep the edges as clean and straight as possible here.

9. Quilt the layers. I quilted with cross stitches spread intermittently over the top, wanting this to look soft.

Detail

10. These two finished pieces were each stretched and mounted on 15" x 17" pieces of foam board.

Baltimore Quilt Project

Finished Size: 49" x 49"

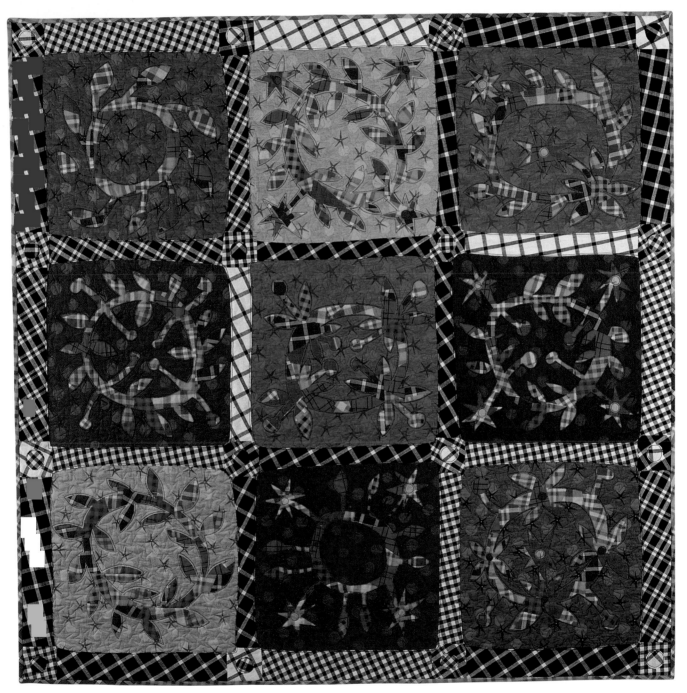

Reversing from Baltimore to Freo by Jan Mullen, 2002

This is a great example of working detailed blocks individually, and fully quilting and finishing them. Later, you can join them together but still form a cohesive whole. The details of this quilt-as-you-go technique are on page 19, along with the instructions needed for the floating sashing on page 20. You will need to familiarize yourself with them.

With its raw edges held only by one row of decorative stitching, my quilt must remain solely in the decorative category. If I wanted to make it functional, I would simply machine stitch the edges with a stitch that covers securely; buttonhole is a good choice.

My secret layer is made up of a bag of plaid off-cuts. I made patchwork covers for our director's chairs and had a pile of trimmings. I love the way the colors mix easily and the directions vary.

I look forward to making the appliqué version of this quilt soon. You, too, will discover this wonderful bonus of using fusible web and a craft blade!

Design

My nine wreaths are all different but made up of the same few components. The wreath, leaves, berries, and stars are common in "real" Baltimore quilts. I combined these elements in a naive manner to achieve a similar effect.

Design components

Fabrics and Threads

Secret layer: approximately 3 yards total assorted yarn-dyed plaid scraps or yardage
Top layer: $1/2$ yard each of 5 tone-on-tone prints

Floating sashing: $1/2$-yard each of 4 black-and-white yarn-dyed plaids
Backing fabric: $1/2$-yard each of 6 yarn-dyed plaids
Batting: Cut 9 squares 16", plus a piece 10" x 52" for the border.
Fusible web: 9 squares 14"
Binding: leftovers or $1/2$ yard total yarn-dyed plaids
Appliqué thread: heavy black top-stitching cotton
Stitching/quilting thread to match top layers

The Process

1. Cutting the blocks: For each of the 9 blocks you will need to cut a 16" square each of backing fabric, batting, and top-layer fabric. Set aside.

2. The secret layer is made from odd-shaped pieces approximately 3" across. You need to stitch these together into pairs, then rows about 16" long. Stitch together enough rows to cover the batting on each of the 9 blocks. Lay the freshly pressed secret layer on the backing/batting sandwich.

3. Draw your designs on each of the 9 squares of fusible web. I do a few thumbnail sketches to warm up, then on the paper side of the web confidently draw the wreath and add some or all of the other components. Try to make them all different and try also to keep it one complete shape. It is a much easier process than it looks. Remember that crooked and quirky is going to be much more effective than equal divisions and symmetry. Another hint: Lightly plot general placements before making more definite lines.

4. Trim the web approximately $1/2$" from the outer edges of the design. Iron these to the center backs of each of the top layer. With a craft blade and mat, very carefully cut on your design lines. If you remove the wreath in one piece you have a bonus appliqué!

5. Remove the paper from the web and position the top layer over the secret layer. Press carefully to secure the edges. Lightly pin the blocks in preparation for the machine appliqué.

6. Using top-stitching thread, appliqué around the raw edges of each wreath, stitching a single line in the top layer about $1/8$" from the edge. I chose to do that for the look, not functionality. I cut some circles from top-layer fabrics to be stitched in the stars; a touch of fusible web helps here, too.

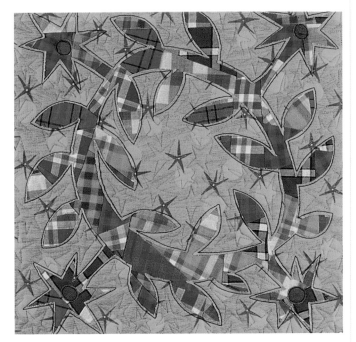

Detail

7. Time to machine quilt. I free-motion quilted stars on each block to hold the sandwich firmly. It is advisable to quilt right to the edge.

8. Trim the blocks to 15" square. Follow the quilt-as-you-go instructions on page 19, Step 5 specifically, to join the blocks.

9. We need to add a batting border around the perimeter to allow for the floating sashing to come.

Cut batting for two side borders 2" x 45" and a top and bottom 2" x 49". Back these and lightly quilt them. Attach these to the quilt with a zigzag stitch as you did to join the blocks. Trim if necessary.

10. Prepare the back sashing as in Step 6 of the quilt-as-you-go instructions. Cut sashings $1^1/2$"-wide and press them to $3/4$". Stitch them to the quilt, covering all seams.

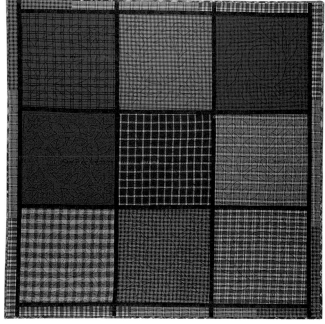

Back sashing

11. Prepare the floating sashing by cutting off-grain: 16 corner squares, each 3" x 3", and 24 strips 3" x 13". Stitch these together to make a hollow frame as in Step 4 on page 21. Pin it to the quilt top as in Step 5.

12. Stitch down the sashing with a single line of top-stitching thread and use a walking foot for extra stability. Finish the design work with a circle of black-and-white plaid stitched in each stop-corner square.

13. The binding can be made from scraps of the secret layer.

Gallery

or postcards from friends

Time to take a peek at what others have been doing. Some of my students, all locals from Western Australia, have taken quick trips and a few have taken the overnight gear. Even with a small selection of samples it is interesting to note that individual styles shine through.

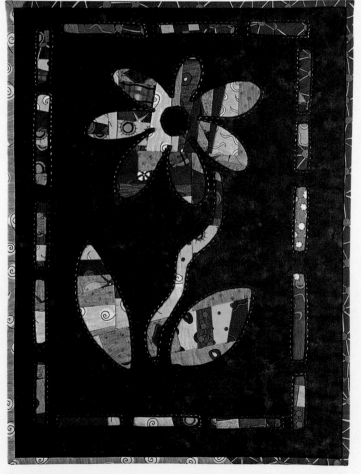

Let's begin with a quilt started in class, a lovely version of my *Daisy Project* on page 53. Kim's border is simple and unusual. It elegantly reveals a bit more of the secret layer.

Funky Flower by Kim Rep,
15" x 20", 2001

Another flower quilt, this time a whole vase full. Jacqui's tulips look quite simple, but she had to plan carefully where the three color fields were placed—no mean feat considering the size of it. I hear that it was a family affair, with hubby involved holding it up to the light!

Indian Summer by Jacqui Macliver,
23" x 52", 2002

Spot the Horse
by Sally Sweetingham,
15" x 11", 2002

Sally's horse is so simple, but the combination of a design with movement, unusual color (non-realistic), and simple naive stitching sets it apart. It makes me smile.

Two darling little creatures now.... Marilyn's bee is not a quilt, but a cushion for her daughter, Melissa. It's in non-realistic bee colors too, so it will fit in Melissa's home. I think this adds to its charm.

The original design was very straight and symmetrical. With a tiny bit of tweaking we skewed him ever so slightly and gave him a broader smile and smaller eyes to take him out of the ordinary bee league.

Melissa's Bee by Marilyn Dillon,
17" x 17", 2002

Katy's Caterpillar by Cindy Taylor,
24" x 27", 2002

When I run workshops in reversing I often supply a small kit containing batting and two interchangeable top layers. In the corner of the room a couple of big baskets sit, full of scraps for my students to use. Having this kit takes the pressure off; there are a few less decisions to be made in the evening. Everyone loves diving into the baskets, coming up for air with hands full.

Cindy came to class with a file of her daughter's drawings. The caterpillar won our affection and the curves could be easily stitched in reverse. When Cindy went diving and came up with a selection of yellows, the discussion turned to piecing them. To get the feel of a caterpillar it needed stripes, but how could we get them following the curves of the body? Wedge shapes were the answer; they are simple to construct and they don't have to be pretty, as the bulk of the fabric is hidden underneath the top layer. So inspired by the wedges was Cindy, that she started thinking (uh oh!) and her second project was conceived; we'll get to that soon. Our time together was a lovely exchange, as I learned that the blanket stitch Cindy used was different from the buttonhole I had thought was the same. Her uneven version is particularly fitting on this critter.

Like the many others who come to class saying they can't draw, Anthea has done wonders tackling a large quilt in a limited time. With a quick lesson on stylizing images, her vision of a farm piece came to fruition.

Many secret layers beg not to be covered and this was one of those, a stunning array of autumn-toned pieces cut from yardage. She sacrificed it to the greater good. Again what looks like a touch of whimsy—what is the crayfish doing in the paddock?—well represents a specialty of the farm, marron (a local variety of fresh-water crayfish). The appliqué is raw-edged and machine stitched.

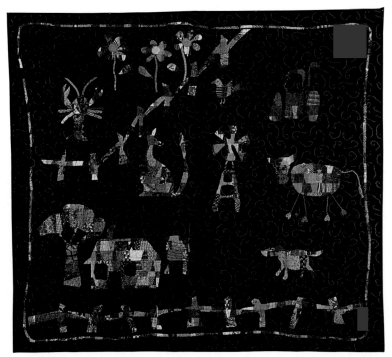

E-I-E-I-O by Anthea Lang,
46" x 42", 2002

Emily's Fairy by Christine Thompson,
28" x 20", 2002

Drawing by Emily Thompson, 16" x 16"

Another daughter was the original artist here and a very particular one too! Young Emily exercised her creative rights to make sure that mum Christine did not sway from the painting. If you look very, very closely at the stripes on the dress you may see that the small brown one near the top is missing; someone noticed! Christine has done a great job with the face, especially where it sits over the hairline attached with a few invisible stitches.

Jack's Mermaid by Melodie Slatter,
8" x 11", 2002

Drawing by Jack Caddy,
15" x 22", 2002

This time a young lad inspired his auntie to go reversing. Melodie used some lovely slinky fabrics in the tail and some pieced pretty pinks for this sweet mermaid's flesh. Instead of piecing the curve of the belly, a simple line of stitching gives us the impression of roundness.

The "Double-D" shells are a great embellishment, covering her more fully. The sort of thing an aunt would do!

 More underwater delights, this time on a bigger scale. Judy started off with an array of sea fabrics and a collection of "cookie-cutter" line drawings. The sea's colors gradated beautifully but would have been a little stilted if it were pieced in straight lines. The curves were achieved by overlapping them from light to dark, then each darker side was marked with the chalk wheel, cut, and machine stitched decoratively. The lighter side was trimmed from underneath. A simple and effective process. The secret layer's gradated color scheme and the lovely contrast between warm creatures in the cool sea works well.

Appliqué was done with decorative machine stitches, too.

Sea Creatures by Judy Stocks,
21" x 35", 2002

 Here we have a gentle, serious piece that shows a great use of fabrics.

Sue had a precious collection of hand-dyed pieces to work with and she has used them to great effect, picking the blotchy bits to suit the design. The cross was proving difficult to coordinate, black being the initial, but not perfect, choice. I sent Sue home with instructions to play with bleach and a few black solids; they should react with various effects.

She hit the jackpot and engineered her own finishing touch to the fully raw-edged piece.

Secrets by Sue Willis, 24" x 24", 2002

Autumn Leaves by Helen Stephens,
24" x 24", 2001

We move on to the last postcard section where the common link is the use of a repeat motif.

Helen is a very skilled stitcher who completed the bulk of this piece in a day class. It isn't easy to make out as the layers are fused beautifully, but under the mottled top layer there are two secret layers, both made up of large pieces. The upper secret layer has been used as a border to the lower leaf form. Luck, or rather, clever use of color, has produced some receding and some pronounced areas. The piecing is surface raw-edged and zigzag stitched. There were some good thoughts flying that day!

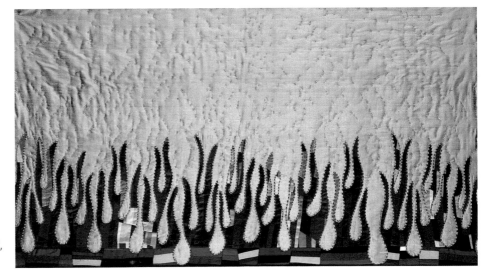

Flames by Julie Howell,
35" x 20", 2002

A collaboration between mum, dad, and Julie resulted in a very unusual fire screen. This lustrous silk piece, though bright in its secret layer, is understated and delicate because of the placement and proportion of the design against the beautifully elegant grey silk. The continuous row of flames looks as though it is hot and flickering; the running stitch and quilting accentuate this.

We had a lot of fun with this next piece as it developed in class. We all came up with different names for this shape, which Bobbie designed on her computer. She rotated it with consummate technical skill and completed the appliqué in invisible machine stitching, something I am not skilled at. Luckily, some of the students come equipped with other fabric experiences.

Doodle Pad by Bobbie Hudd,
29" x 29", 2002

Checkered Out by Tracey Marsegaglia,
32" x 32", 2002

Tracey set herself a challenge with this one! She started with a strong vision and it was a matter of trying to match that with new skills, a busy life, and white fabric. Luckily she was flexible. A checkers game is underway with the playing pieces, the checkers themselves, on the black and white board. The checkers are beautifully detailed with the wedge idea (see *Kathy's Caterpillar* on page 72), being used in a different effect here. As an upper secret layer, bordering a circle underneath, it subtly frames the checkers. She answered her challenge to produce a striking piece.

Back to Cindy again to show you how the wedge thought developed. This was yet another quilt with a secret layer that didn't want to be relegated to second place. It is a full layer made of crooked Kaleidoscope blocks, predominately in striped fabric. The center of each star is the center of some, but not all of the blocks. The top layer is a beautiful frame to them; the borders help to create a focus in this repeat pattern without being too formal.

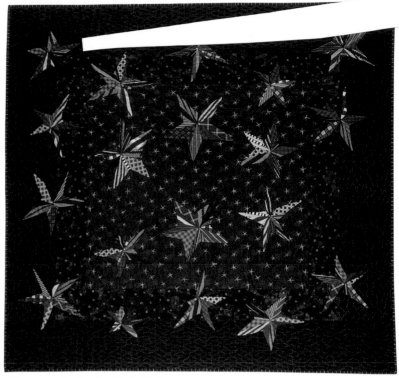

Stargazey Gazing by Cindy Taylor,
54" x 57", 2002

 I thought we'd finish the visuals close to where we started. *We walk a crooked line* is that "one-good-quilt-deserves-another" quilt, made the same way and with similar fabrics to my first. The border freedom especially is a real bonus with this technique, it still pleases me a few years later.

We walk a crooked line by Jan Mullen,
39$^{1}/_{2}$" x 59", 1998

CONCLUSION

or engine off

 Hope you're not feeling too overwhelmed or carsick. I've given you a lot to think about, haven't I?

By now your mind is probably filled with images of wondrous fabrics, threads, and new processes. Your imagination must be racing with grand designs, and your fingers are twitching with desire!

You have a full information tank. Use it to make choices in your own projects, as you will undoubtedly face some tricky corners where you are not sure of the correct direction. I can't be with you to navigate, so if in doubt about which way to proceed, idle a while, or take a step back (reverse!), and keep your ideas and thoughts simple.

SUPPLIES

For an interesting array of threads online:

THE THREAD STUDIO
6 Smith Street
Perth, Western Australia 6000
Phone: (08) 9227 1561
Fax: (08) 9227 0254
www.thethreadstudio.com
mail@thethreadstudio.com

For information about where to obtain Jan Mullen fabric:

MARCUS BROTHERS TEXTILES, INC.
980 Avenue of the Americas
New York, NY 10018
Phone: 212-354-8700 or 1-800-548-8295
Fax: 212-354-5245 or 1-800-548-8296
www.marcusbrothers.com

For wholesale threads, tools, and Stargazey patterns;

QUILTERS' RESOURCE
P.O. Box 148850 Chicago IL 60614
Phone: 1-800-676-6543 or 1-773-278-5695
Fax: 1-800-216-2374 or 1-773-278-1348
www.quiltersresource.com

For more information, write for a free catalog:

C&T PUBLISHING, INC.
P.O. Box 1456
Lafayette, CA 94549
(800) 284-1114
Email: ctinfo@ctpub.com
Website: www.ctpub.com

For quilting supplies:

COTTON PATCH MAIL ORDER
3405 Hall Lane, Dept.CTB
Lafayette, CA 94549
(800) 835-4418
(925) 283-7883
Email:quiltusa@yahoo.com
Website: www.quiltusa.com

Note: Fabrics used in the quilts shown may not be currently available since fabric manufacturers keep most fabrics in print for only a short time.

A Bit About Jan

Contact Jan at:
Stargazey Quilts
9-100 Stirling Highway
North Fremantle
Western Australia, 6159
Phone: +61 8 9433 3129
fax +61 8 9433 3109

jan@stargazey.com
www.stargazey.com

Jan loves her work but is very happy in her time at home. She sees a bit more of it when not writing books! Domestic bliss reigns when the oven is full, her four darlings—Ben, Brodie, Keelan, and Miffy—are at home with the music up loud, and the two hairy ones, Celeste and Rocket, are on their rugs.

A long time ago she did the proper thing and gained a B. Ed (Art/Craft) majoring in textiles and sculpture. This qualification assures her that she's passing on her wicked ideas to willing students in the correct manner.

Her varied working life as owner of Stargazey Quilts enables her to travel, produce lots of crooked quilt patterns, and design copious amounts of bright fabric. Getting out the paints and playing with color in a messy medium is a real treat, especially when the paintings come boomeranging back in the form of fabric.

She'd love to say that she enjoys lots of adventurous pursuits like sky diving, but the weekly Monday night movie date with her man, or a pile of magazines with coffee and a chokky (chocolate) are the much-anticipated high points in her life at the moment.

INDEX